"You" by Ricky Roberts III

Published in the United States of America
by Tate Publishing, LLC
127 East Trade Center Terrace
Mustang, OK 73064
(888) 361-9473

ISBN: 0-9752572-8-5

YOU

Author: Ricky Roberts III

TATE PUBLISHING, LLC

Table of Contents

Introduction

This book came to me at a time in my life when a lot of "things" were in question. I was confused about my life and the direction it was heading. I felt alone, lost, and defeated. I began to search within myself. I had to understand what it was that I was feeling. So I began to spend a lot of my time alone, and most importantly, I began to write. I began to think about what was bothering me and what I truly wanted for "me." I thought about what it was that I would want to tell someone in my shoes - what I wish someone would have told me as a child or even in general.

I did not write this with the intention of providing answers to one's problems or to imply that my views and thoughts are the only way. I wrote with the intentions of helping someone. I wanted to be able to work through my confusion while at the same time give someone else a chance to read what it was that I did and what I thought about to understand myself and what I did to overcome my own barriers. I know there are so many things that come up in our lives - so many forks in the road, and so many decisions that need to be made. Where do you turn in all of this? What if you have no one to turn to? What if you feel like no one understands you?

First off, my strength comes from lifting it all up to God and turning to him for guidance. Aside from that, you need to dig deep inside of yourself and try to understand what it is that you want out of life. As I was analyzing my life and determining what is important and what is not, I began to work through many issues. I began to think about all of the things that I have overcome in my life. Then I couldn't help but think about how nice it would have been to have had some guidance from someone. That brings me to this book. I was moved to express my feelings and share my outlook on life and what it means to me. I had to give you what I was giving myself.

I hope that you are able to gain something from reading this. Do not read it looking for answers, read it with an open mind allowing it to stimulate thoughts in your life that need to be discovered. Everything within this book is sincere and from my heart. Open your mind and listen to the things that you may need to hear.

YOU

When life feels like it is passing you by, stop and reflect. Take the time to analyze your views on life and your attitude toward "it." Life is a frame of mind you put yourself in. Things happen in life, which are out of our control, but we choose how we deal with them. Everyone has the ability to make the best out of life no matter what happens to him or her.

As a youngster, I was labeled as a punk-skateboarder, troublemaker, and a loser, who was going nowhere in life. Moreover, I was not encouraged to go anywhere in my life. Statistics would point out that someone with my experiences would end up in jail, killed, or strung out on drugs. I have overcome many adversities. I have accomplished things in my life that never seemed possible. My drive to succeed will take me as far as I want to go in my life. It's simple; it's all in my attitude. I am where I am at today because I chose to be here. We all have a choice.

Adversities and setbacks cannot stand in the way of your dreams. Nothing makes you any different from the person that has accomplished what you want to accomplish. "It" has to be in you. It is all about you. YOU are responsible for what YOU make of your LIFE. It is all too easy for us to settle, to let the unfortunate situations in which we are placed to hold us down. We let the negativity in our lives consume us and chain us down to the nearest comfort spot. Move forward. Use the set backs as fuel to catapult you to higher levels of growth and understanding. Allow yourself to become wiser and stronger. Grow with time; do not let time pass you by.

Dreams begin inside. It is up to us to make them our reality. A dream is just a dream if it is not pursued. Dig deep inside of yourself. Ask yourself if you are doing everything you can to get more fulfillment out of life. What truly makes "you" happy? What do you want out of your life? With enough will, determination, and God's grace, anything and everything is possible.

Life Is All About Choices

When bad things happen to people, in many cases, they choose to feel sorry for themselves. They give up. They tend to settle. So often you hear people complain about all of their problems and make excuses for why they are where they are. For example, many people hate their jobs and have bigger dreams for themselves and yet do nothing about it. The majority of people feels sorry for themselves and complains about their lives.

We live in a society that requires maximum effort accompanied by a great deal of determination. The beauty is that there are so many opportunities in our country; it's just a matter of knowing what you want and going after it.

Whatever you want to be, whatever you want to get out of your life, go for it. You can do it. You are probably thinking, "Yeah right, it is so much easier said than done." Not true. Do not accept that statement. It is just a matter of knowing what you want and making the necessary choices and sacrifices to get "it." Get what you want out of your life. Live the life you want for you. It has to all be for you. Others can benefit from your decisions, but ultimately, it is you who has to live with the way you feel inside. Feel good about yourself. Do not sell yourself short on anything you do in your life.

The people amongst us who are living the life we want for ourselves, are the people who know what they want and set their goals to make their dreams come true. They have problems, setbacks, and difficulties, too. Naturally, it may be easier for some than others. There will always be people who are better off than you, who seem to have things so much easier. This is a given. It is life. Don't feel sorry for yourself. Someone always has it better, and someone always has it worse. Thank God you have "it" - LIFE. If one has the desire and the drive despite the obstacles life brings, the sky is the limit. Reach for the stars!

Life is full of obstacles; it's just a matter of how you deal with them that matters most.

There are many different ways people handle life's setbacks: The people who give up, the people who ignore their problems, the people who have a break down, the people who blame others or question why it is happening to them, and then you have the "ones" who seek knowledge and change through their troubles. This is what makes us individuals. Despite how bad things may be, we still have a choice as to how we deal with our lives. We may not be able to choose what happens to us but we can choose how we handle what happens to us.

These differences among us are what determines whether one settles or whether one seeks change and desires more for themselves. Take my family for example. There were six of us. I have three brothers and two sisters. My mother was a single parent left alone to fend for herself and six of us after surviving a twelve-year abusive relationship with my father.

Unfortunately, we witnessed many of the violent outbreaks by my father. Let me give you one example to get a better understanding of who he was at the time. One day we were leaving his boss's house after a barbeque. He and my mother were fighting of course. My mother must have said something wrong. The next thing I knew my father hit my mom in the face, slowed down the car, and threw her out while it was still moving. We were all begging him to go back and pick her up. He drove for a while and finally went back to get her. No apologies or nothing just screaming and yelling all the way home. It was torture to watch my mother be treated the way she was by him.

It got to the point where the drugs and alcohol began to rule his life and ours more and more. His drug use began to increase, not only how much he was doing, but how many kinds he was doing. I remember on my tenth or eleventh birthday walking in on my father doing crack cocaine. He promised he would not do it again but was out on a weekend long binge that following week. The violence and abuse got worse. It was the norm to see my Dad drunk or drugged up. We never knew when he would explode. Finally, he and my mother had a final blow out, and he took off. Several years went by before I heard from him. He abandoned us. We lost everything. Most of our belongings were left behind when my Mom lost the house and we had to move. We went from a three bedroom two bathroom house with a pool to a one bedroom apartment.

While it was a relief to not be exposed to the actions of my father or have the fear of what would happen next, it was painful to not have a father in my life. From about age twelve on I knew no other way but to fend for myself. My older brother moved in with my uncle Bob when everything blew apart. I was the oldest in the house. I had to be strong for my mother, younger brothers, and sisters. I had to be the man of the house. It got tuff for my mother to support six kids. There were times when we did not know where we would live, if we would eat, if we would have electricity, or warm water to take a shower. Moving from house to house became common practice.

I do not blame my mother. I know she did what she could, given the circumstance. She is a fighter! Even though we hit rock bottom more than once, my mother always found a way, it may not have always been the best way, but we always found a way. I look back on my life now and realize how big of a part God was in it all along. He was always there when we needed him most.

Anyway, we all grew up in the same environment and were exposed to the same negative experiences. Although we all had similar experiences, we all were affected by them differently. Each one of us dealt with the circumstances in a different way. Each of our reactions are reflected by where each one of us are in our lives. Each one of us can choose what outlook we take and what decisions we make in our lives.

As a child, I began to develop my own outlook on life. I decided at a young age that I would not let anything hold me down. I would not let a rough childhood stand in the way of what I wanted out of life. I would not be held back by circumstance. I would not be a product of my environment. I would not let anyone tell me I could not do it. I would not be convinced by the ones coaching me to settle for the "that's just the way it is" mentality. I would break out of the chains. I would pave my own future. I knew nothing in this life is easy and nothing is free. Most importantly, I have known all along that it is up to each individual to make his or her life what he or she wants it to be. One cannot rely on anyone else for his or her happiness. Each person must do it for himself.

Everything Happens For A Reason

Everything happens for a reason. Everything that each one of us goes through is planned to make us who we are meant to be as a person. God has a plan for everything. He gives us our obstacles to make us who we are destined to be; everyone has his or her place in this world. One will never find his or her true self unless he or she is willing to seek knowledge and growth through life's tragedies. Every experience good, bad, or indifferent is meant to help us grow as individuals.

Take an episode I had as a youth for example. At the age of seventeen, I was a person filled with anger and hostility. At the time the only way I knew how to deal with confrontation was in a negative or violent way. This brings me to the "Night," the Epiphany of my life.

I was out with some friends one night. I had to work the next morning, so I had planned on going in early. My friends dropped me off at home. At the last second, I decided to stay out. They were driving away when I called out to them to wait for me. I was being led out that night. We went to Y-Bor City, a place filled with dance clubs and bars about twenty minutes from home. It was a popular place to go.

My friends Chris, Scott, and I (there were others, but they were not directly involved) were standing on the street "people watching" when these two kids walked up, and one of them asked if we had a problem with their girlfriend (who was yelling at us from across the street). He made an attempt to swing at my friend Scott. Scott punched him in the face before the kid could hit him. I clocked the kid next to him, and Chris began to fight with a kid that came from across the street. Before we knew it, kids were coming at us from every direction. Apparently, they had mistaken us for another group of guys and had set the whole thing up. Fists were flying, beer bottles busting, and screams screeching. As seconds went by, the situation got worse. We were completely out numbered.

I got backed up against a wall by a group of about ten guys and a couple of girls; with no other choice, I ran directly at the kids swinging with everything I had. I truly was fighting for my life. As I fought through the group, one of them grabbed my shirt; it began to rip off. As it was being pulled off, I felt something piercing into my back. I continued to fight my way through the mob. Finally, I was out of the pack. I looked down and saw that I was missing a shoe, had no shirt, and was completely covered in blood. At that point I realized that something serious had happened. When your body is raging with adrenaline and you are fighting for survival, you don't comprehend exactly what is happening. I walked away in a daze.

I found Scott first. He was holding his stomach with his hands covered in blood; it was cut open from one side to the other. We could see the fear in each other's eyes. At that point we both knew we were in serious condition. As we stumbled away, a man walked up and offered us a ride to the hospital. Scott got in the car with him. I did not choose to get in the car with him; I was in shock trying to get a grasp of what had just happened.

I wandered for a minute and found my friend James who drove us there in the first place. He helped us out in the fight but escaped with no wounds; he was on the outskirts of the situation. He put me in the car; we then realized Chris was missing. We started driving on the sidewalks looking for him in complete panic. Meanwhile, I was gushing out blood everywhere, totally freaking out. It was like a scene out of a movie. We spotted Chris in a doorway; he was laying there with his finger in his stab wound trying to slow down the bleeding. We got him into the car and continued to drive.

We found a police officer in a parking lot just up the road. Chris fell out of the car, and James helped me over to the officer to get him to call the ambulance. It seemed like eternity before the ambulance finally got there. My friend and I lay there thinking death was around the corner. It was hard to breathe and everything was getting dark. I felt like I was dying. I was lying there holding my eyes open with the fear that if they closed, I would be dead. I was very afraid; I did not want to die. Eventually, two ambulances arrived and rushed us to the hospital.

The second I arrived to the hospital I was mobbed by doctors and nurses. They began to shove tubes and needles in me everywhere. With me seeing the concern in their eyes increased my level of fear even more. I knew things were not good. The doctors and nurses knew I was stabbed but could not tell where because of all the blood. I even heard someone in the distance trying to get a hold of my mother in fear that I would not make it through the night; I was losing a lot of blood.

As I was lying in the hospital staring up at the bright lights and the eyes of the doctors and nurses, seeing the intensity in their eyes, the hospital Chaplain came into the room. He walked over to me through all the commotion. He placed his hand on my head; I looked up at him as he looked down at me. He said, "Everything is going to be okay son." The whole room seemed to stop, and peace filled my whole body. It was a sense of peace that I had never felt before. It touched my soul. From that moment on, I knew I was going to live through the experience. I knew I was not alone. I laid there in peace for about seven hours as they scrubbed my wounds and stitched me up. Granted, I was in serious pain physically, but spiritually I was at peace knowing that God was with me and that he is real. I felt his realness in my heart.

I chose to seek knowledge and growth from the experience I had that night. I knew there was something to be learned, or should I say plenty to be learned. There is so much to be learned in every experience in your life. The most important thing I learned on that fearful night is that I am not alone. God is real; that night supported my belief in God very strongly. I knew when the Chaplin put his hand on my head that God was with me; it was not my time.

Another lesson I learned was that I needed to change my outlook on life. Life is too precious to waste away with the wrong outlook. Keeping a positive outlook on life makes things so much more enjoyable. I made changes in my life. Being stabbed nine-times across my body and staring death in the face was one of the worst things to happen to me, but yet, at the same time, it was one of the best things to happen to me as well. This could have just been a tragic experience if I did not seek emotional, mental, and spiritual growth from it all. "Seek and YOU Shall Find."

Although I chose to seek knowledge and growth from this tragic experience I am not sure what Chris and Scott took from the episode. I do know that both of them are doing very well. Unfortunately, we never got a chance to talk about how this incident affected our lives. We all survived but walked away in different directions. After I began my physical and psychological recovery, I started to drift away from Scott and

Chris. It was not because of anything they did wrong. I knew I had to focus on growing. Changing my surroundings happened to be one of the steps that I needed to take in order to do so.

No matter what circumstances one may endure, there is always a lesson to be learned. The key to moving forward in life is to seek understanding and knowledge through life's experiences. Whether it be good or bad, big or small, ask yourself, "What can I learn from this experience?" The more you seek knowledge, growth, and understanding, the broader your horizons will be.

Our minds are one of the most powerful tools available to us. The more you push "it" the stronger "it" gets. Never stop pushing yourself; you have no limits.

We Set Our Own Limits

There are endless opportunities in the world in which we live. I would say that there are more opportunities in this world than we will ever take advantage of. Whatever success means to you, there is plenty of opportunity for you to reach it. We set our own limits. We decide what satisfies us in life. Some people get to a certain level of accomplishment, accept where they have gotten to, and stop. In most instances it is not because they are where they want to be in life, rather it is that they are settling for where they are in life. People coast along at their comfort level. In fact, they convince themselves that they are satisfied. Then later on in life they will struggle with the feeling of regret - wishing that they would have gotten more out of there life and realizing more was possible than they believed. More so, people may get bored with their accomplishments, wishing they would have chosen a different path, like they did not get enough out of their lives. It is never too late! The bottom line is that there are so many of us who are unfulfilled with our choices in life but do nothing to change or move forward.

The fear of the unstable and unknown can be overwhelming. I ask you to take the time to reflect, dig deep, listen, convince yourself within, and do not stop until you are completely satisfied within. The emphasis is on "YOU." You have to make yourself happy before you can make others happy. Do not take your decisions in life lightly. This is your chance, the opportunity to get out of life what you desire. Set goals! Chase YOUR dreams! Do not be intimidated or discouraged. Try hard and never stop. Obstacles you will face, BUT obstacles you will overcome.

Change

There is one way to overcome the dissatisfaction one may feel in his or her life, CHANGE. One must seek change. The ways of change are plentiful. You must be willing to push your limits - at least the limits that you think you have. Either consciously or unconsciously we set limits for ourselves. A person's boundaries are set by no one except himself. People will tell you anything you let them tell you. "You can't do that." "That is not right." "There is no way." "Who you? Yeah right." "Are you sure you want to try that? What if you fail?" etc... Ultimately your expectations and limits for "YOU" are up to only you. You are the one responsible for your life. You set your own boundaries. Granted, God has a plan. He may put obstacles in your path, but you still have the choice as to how you handle them.

You have to be willing to take risks and push your expectations of yourself further than what they are now. Professional athletes for example, never stop pushing themselves. Even when they are at the top of their domain, they still continue to push their boundaries. They never stop pushing. Once they accomplish one goal they strive for another.

If a running back breaks a record of most yards per game, he will push for more yards the next game and more after that. Years ago, a BMX jumper would have been happy with executing a 360 over a dirt jump. Now they are doing double back flips. The list goes on - surfers, skateboarders, basketball players, etc... Those athletes are taking their skills to unbelievable levels. The point is that if these athletes settled, the bar would not be pushed day in and day out. They are always trying to push to new heights. These individuals have the drive to constantly overcome new boundaries. Whether you are a professional athlete or not, we all have the capabilities to possess that drive to move us forward in life. It is up to us to push ourselves to the next level. No matter if you're learning to play the drums, opening a business, or seeking higher education. Go for "it;" know no boundaries.

Change does not start by talking about it. "It" starts by doing it. Not tomorrow, not next week, or even next year, change starts today. What do I do? How do I begin? Take inventory of your life. Take an honest approach to what makes you happy, what makes you unhappy, what you are satisfied with, and what you are not satisfied with. Then think of the things that would make your life more pleasing. Set goals with time frames as to when you want to accomplish them. Design a plan. Although change starts when you choose it to, one important thing to keep in mind is that it does not happen overnight. In fact, change is a lifelong process that keeps us moving forward. Grow with time. Do not let time pass you by. You must decide what you want out of life and constantly take steps toward achieving those things.

It Is All About YOU

While it is important to benefit others, such as your family and close friends, it has to begin with "YOU." The most important person you need to worry about making happy is "YOU." Be true to yourself. Only doing things for others, will never make you happy. Seek your own happiness, and you will make plenty of other people happy.

So many people take on someone else's goals for themselves, instead of focusing on their own. For example, take a father who's always telling his son or daughter he or she is going to be a doctor someday - "just like him." His child buys into the idea and chooses the dream of the father as his own. That dream would fulfill the father's desire, but it does not mean the child would have the same desires for him or herself without all the pressure from the father. Do not take on ideas other people have for you. You will not be completely fulfilled. Your fulfillment has to come from within. You know what you want for yourself. Dig deep and know yourself. Seeking those deep desires will bring you more happiness than the desires someone else or the society may have for you. You have to do things for yourself when you are chasing your dreams. Your motivation and determination will be much stronger than you could ever imagine when you are doing what feels right for you.

Understand, I am not implying that you should not be concerned with other people's opinions or advice. That is not the case at all. The point I am trying to make is that you need to always keep sight of your own goals and dreams. Stay in touch with your aspirations. Do not loose the vision of what you will get for "YOU." When it comes down to the bottom line, you are the one that will live with your choices that you make in your life. Others can compliment you and enjoy your achievements, but ultimately "YOU" are the one that lives with what it feels like inside. Do not buy that nice car because it impresses your neighbors; buy that car because it impresses you. Do not be a lawyer because your family will praise you for it and society will respect you for "it;" be a lawyer because it is your passion to be one. Do everything with passion. Passion comes from within. It is only there if what you are doing in your life, for your life, with your life, and about your life is coming from within.

The passion within brings joy to your life. Trying to impress others and fulfill others expectations of you, may bring joy to them, but will leave you feeling lost, unsatisfied, and empty. Remember, you are the one who has to live with "you!"

Setting Goals

Setting goals is one of the most important elements of forward motion. Set your goals high. Do not sell yourself short. There are many types of goals. Short term, long term, and ultimate goals are how I like to categorize them. Goal setting has to come from within. You have to believe in the goals you set. Goals are marker points in your life that you desire to meet. They bring fulfillment through the satisfaction of making forward progress. Keep in mind that it is okay to start small.

Before I continue, let me give you a brief description as to how I define short term, long term, and ultimate goals.

Short-term goals are things you want to accomplish in the near future. These are goals that allow you to make steps toward your long term goals.

Long-term goals are focuses you have on your future, such as buying a house within two years, being done with school in four years, etc...

Your short and long term goals are always active. You should always have goals you are working toward. Goals stimulate motivation, motivation brings success, and success brings fulfillment. Once again, it has to be your success. What success is to one person, may not be success to another.

Ultimate goals can be defined by where you ultimately see yourself or what you see yourself ultimately achieving. This is what drives your short and long term goals. This is what you want "it" all to amount to. It is the big picture - the light at the end of the tunnel. For example, I have many goals both short and long term. They are the goals I am using to bring me to my ultimate goals in life. All of my short and long term goals will amount to a life of enjoyment, joy, growth, change, achievement, satisfaction, freedom, a wonderful family, and to have made a difference along the way. I will be able to look back on my life and feel good about the things I have done and the people I have helped. Moreover, I want to pass my legacy on to many generations to come. Through my successes, I will spread good seed. I will have more than financial success. I will make it possible for my kids (when I have them) to be able to enjoy a life I only dreamed of as a child. To change the cycle I was placed in and to give my children a life of joy and happiness is one of my deepest desires, not just on a materialistic level, but on a spiritual and emotional level as well. This is my fuel.

You may be thinking, what about your goals needing to be for you. I say, my goals are for me and me alone. Accomplishing the desires I have within will make me truly happy. I desire these things for me. However, others may benefit from me reaching them, but it is me who will feel the deep pleasure of accomplishing what I want for myself. I will break the pattern that I was expected to follow.

Now, back to setting goals. Make a list of things you want out of life. What brings you joy? What kind of life do you want to maintain? What is happiness to you? Imagine where you see yourself a year from now, five years from now, and even twenty years from now. Determine what you want to change about the direction in which your life is going. Decide what is important to "YOU." Make a list of things you want to accomplish. Categorize them under short term, long term, and ultimate goals or anyway you see fit. Make goals for a month away, a year away, even five years away; just make some goals.

By making goals for yourself and making them a part of your lifestyle, you will begin to feel purpose in your life. Feeling purpose in your life is a great motivational tool. Remember, "YOU" can do anything if "YOU" have enough determination. Set your goals high; do not settle.

An important thing to keep in mind while pursuing your goals is that there are things that happen in our lives, which are out of our control.

If you set a goal to achieve in a years time and you do not reach it for two years, don't be discouraged. Most importantly, don't give up. Stay focused on your dreams. Do not ever lose sight of them. Also remember God has a plan for everything, and our plan is not always what is best for us at the time. It is all in his timing.

I think of it like this: If you are walking down a dark road with a light straight ahead of you off in the distance, you focus on that light to guide you through the darkness. Along the way there will be curves, hurdles, dips, bumps, hills (which seem like up hill most of the time), puddles, and solid walls. As long as you keep your focus on that light, you will reach it. Your goals are the same way. Focus on what you want, do not lose focus. If you fall down, keep looking ahead, get back up, brush yourself off, and continue toward the light. Never lose sight no matter where the road takes you.

Never Let Anyone Tell You that You Cannot

Do not listen to the negative people who try to tell you that you can't do something, for example: "That is impossible." "What if you fail?" "That is too risky." "Why don't you…" "You should be a…" "You spend too much time on that." "It is all about security." "Bla bla bla bla bla…" You get the picture.

Anyone who tells you that you cannot do something may not be satisfied with his or her own accomplishments. It is very possible that he or she harbors bitterness from failure. This person gave up; hence, he or she tells you that something is not possible. Just because someone else gave up on his or her dreams does not mean you should let them discourage you from living yours.

If a man can walk on the moon, if you can play a video game with someone in China from your own home thousand of miles away, if a man can do a back flip on a motorcycle, and if an athlete can do a 900 degree turn on a skateboard in mid air, then anything is possible. The list of men and women who have achieved outstanding and unbelievable things can go on infinitely. Think of all of those amazing individuals and their accomplishments and imagine if they had listened to someone telling them they could not do "it."

If I had bought into the discouragement of others that was coming form every angle you would not be reading this book right now. It was so funny for me to see and hear the reactions I got from people when I told them that I was writing a book. They looked at me like, "Who you? Write a book? Yeah, right." Very few people seemed to give me the credit of being capable of accomplishing such a thing. Then after I finished and talked about getting my book published, the responses were even more negative. The only thing most people seemed to talk about was how hard it is to get a book published and never that what I wrote may have the potential of reaching that point of publication. Even if "they" did not come right out and say that they did not believe in me, I saw it in their eyes and heard it in their reactions to my excitement about what I was accomplishing. I continuously heard comments like: "So many people try to get a book published; they never make it and a publisher will not give you the time of day."

Before I continue, I must say that there were those few who did encourage me and did believe in me. I am very grateful for those people. Regardless of how many people tell you that you cannot do something, there will be the select few who encourage you to chase your dreams. Keep those people close to your heart and always be thankful for the ones who support you.

Anyway, despite the lack of support and enduring the spoken doubts of others, I stayed focused, believed in myself, and trusted God. I knew it would be hard, but I continued to chase my ambitions and prayed for God to open the doors for me if he wanted to use this book to reach others. You are reading an example of my "not listening to people telling me that I can not."

Our society is full of negative people. Prove them wrong; prove them all wrong. Use their negativity as your fuel. It brings me great joy to achieve something that someone told me I could not. Not just for the mere fact of proving them wrong, but because of knowing that I can believe enough in myself to accomplish things I desire. Getting encouragement from others is very helpful. However, I know if I believe in myself then that is what matters the most. It feels great to prove people wrong by doing something you knew you could do all along. Remember it is in YOU. Believe it is in YOU. You need to make your dreams come true.

As one of six children, in a single parent low-income home, I was exposed to many negative circumstances as well as violent situations. I had no stability and very little in the way of discipline. I spent a great deal of my time on the streets skateboarding, which by the way was the glue that held me together. I was forced to learn a lot of things the hard way. I learned a lot from the streets. I stayed out as late as possible to avoid being home. I was on the streets more at age fourteen than some will ever be. Statistics would show mostly bad outcomes of a child being raised in the environment in which I grew up. Even in elementary school and middle school I had people discouraging me, saying, "I would be a failure" and that "I would be like the rest of them." The rest of them refers to everyone else who came before me in my family that did nothing with their lives and the people of my stereotype that had no desire to move forward in their lives - no positive direction. What people did not know is that I had my direction burning inside of me. With Gods blessing, I knew I would break the cycle in which I was caught.

Do me a favor. Clear your mind. Listen very closely. This is very important. I have seen more bad things at age twenty-six than most will ever see in their lifetime. I have been exposed to enough craziness to make one question everything, especially life. I am not implying that I have had it worse than anyone else. What I am saying is that no matter how bad things are, you can overcome them. I have had to overcome great obstacles in all aspects of my life. I am no different from YOU. It is inside of you. DIG deep. Find your strength. Have faith; God will give you the wisdom and courage you need to move forward. You must dig for it. Seek understanding out of all of your turmoil. YOU CAN DO IT! There is nothing that makes me (or anyone else) different from you. Find the fire inside. If I can break the chains, then so can you.

There is a specific experience that plays out in my head that I would like to share with you. I was in high school, a skateboarder of course, when I had a teacher call me outside the classroom at the end of a semester, and say, "Ricky, when you walked into my classroom I never expected you to pass this class, and I thought that you would do nothing but cause trouble." He apologized for his prejudices and stereotyping. Turns out, I was one of his best students. Basically, he thought I would be nothing but trouble because of my appearance and the fact that I was a skateboarder.

Another thing I remember that I always got a kick out of was going to the Honor Roll breakfast (all A's, B's, and no more than one C). People would always ask how I sneaked in. I got in there from maintaining over a 3.5 Grade Point Average. However, because of my appearance and what people thought I was like, I had to sneak in. Inside my head, I laughed at their shallowness thinking to myself, "You have no clue who I am and what I will be."

There are times when I feel like standing on a podium and screaming, "Look at me now!!" - not just from a financial or materialistic standpoint, but also from a psychological, spiritual, and emotional standpoint. The point I am trying to make, if it is not yet clear, is that no matter what anyone thinks, what a statistic may show, or what a person may say to discourage you; do not let it hold you down. Prove them all wrong for "YOU." Believe!

Surround Yourself With Positive People

You do not have a choice as to how people will act towards you. You cannot control whether or not someone encourages or discourages you. You cannot control what someone's direction may be for himself or herself. You have no control over those who stereotype you or underestimate you. However, you can control with whom you spend your time. If there is one saying I would totally agree with, it is "You are who you hang out with." It is very important to surround yourself with positive people. They need to be encouraging, and it definitely helps for them to have direction in their own lives. It does not have to be the same direction as yours, but there must be a direction. You do not need anyone, especially friends, holding you back.

You have to choose your friends wisely. Take notice of your friends' views about things and their goals for themselves. Friends can be the best or worst things for progress. If you have friends that only think about partying, partying, and some more partying, then chances are that those friends have no serious goals and will to move forward with their lives. More than likely, they will hold you back. I am not saying whether you should or should not party or that there is anything wrong with it if you do. Moreover, I am not saying you cannot enjoy yourself. There must be a balance. There has to be more to life than partying. You have to prioritize and recognize what you want out of life. Some people are totally content with not having any direction and forward motion, but you are not…

As I continued to grow, I had to take inventory of the people with whom I surrounded myself. The sad thing is that a majority of my friends did not have the same interest in growing and progressing as I did. As a matter of fact, I realized that most of what a majority of my friends and I had in common were our younger days and the common interests we once had. This is a very difficult time in my life, but a very enlightening time as well. I went from having a large group of friends with whom I spent a large amount of time, to very few close friends. The friends I choose to stay in contact with on a regular basis are positive influences on my growth. We do not have the same goals or desires, but what we do have in common is direction. These are friends that can appreciate my drive in life. They motivate me. They support me and inspire me by their desire to chase their own dreams. While it was a challenge to not feel as social as I once was, it was a good thing to realize who my friends for life are.

Understand, I am not saying that you have to lose all contact with friends that do not have dreams or goals for themselves; just be aware of the negative influences that they can have on you. Limit your time with them. They can hold you down. As scary and hard as it may be, evaluate your friends with your life in mind.

You must understand that I completely realize how scary this seems to be. It was very scary for me to start spending time alone; I was so comfortable with my friends. We grew up together. I relied on them for who I was. I could not do anything unless we were all doing something together. As much as I dislike saying it, I depended on everyone else but myself. I was who I was hanging out with and what they expected me to be. As I began to spend time alone and open up to people that I normally would not have (because they were not who "the group" would except), I started to see more of who I was. I also began to realize that my thoughts were not my own, but were the influenced thoughts of the people with whom I surrounded myself.

Unfortunately, most of the thoughts and actions that I was buying into were not going to help me become the person I desired to be. I spent more and more time alone and started to know myself. I blossomed more each day into the person I am today. I am proud of who "I" am. It is a wonderful feeling to know that you are your own person. I can honestly say from the deepest part of my heart and soul that taking the time to change who I was and having the courage to step away from my negative surroundings is one of the best things I ever did and ever could have done for myself.

Take the time to give yourself the gift of individuality; you will fall in love with "YOU." This is not an overnight process so be patient with yourself and trust God. He will guide you and will open your eyes up to a part of yourself you never imagined being there. You owe this beauty to yourself! Also, understand that this is a lifelong process, so always be open to knowing yourself deeper than you did yesterday.

I still see my old group of friends from time to time but, I do not make a strong effort to do so. The funny thing is that when I do see them, they are still living in the same mindset and lifestyle we were in years ago. The depth of our conversation is shallow. Part of a friendship is conversation. I no longer have an interest in having the same level of conversation we had five years ago - no real stimulating and mind provoking conversation. There are a lot of things I wish to understand in my life and the world around me.

You may find that all of your friends are anchors to your progress. If you do, do not get discouraged, God will send you more. There will be people you will meet who will be a positive part of your life. In your time alone, focus on your own personal growth. Find yourself. Timing is everything! It may get lonely at times, but in the end it will be well worth the sacrifices. "YOU" are worth every sacrifice you will make to get what you want out of your life.

Convince Yourself Within

The sacrifices you make today are very minor compared to the joy you will get out of achieving what you want in life. Not only do you have to believe in yourself, you have to convince yourself within. Know that what you want to achieve in life is possible. Overcome the doubts that are harbored inside of you. Once you have convinced yourself in mind, body, soul, and spirit; let your journey begin. Keep in mind that you cannot convince other people that your dreams are possible. You do not need to worry about convincing anyone but yourself anyhow. By convincing yourself your accomplishment will come. Think of an activist fighting for a cause he or she truly believes in versus an activist who fights for a cause that he or she does not belief in whole-heartedly. The ones who fight for something they truly believe in, stand a much greater chance of being successful with their purposes. Their actions will display their sincere belief in what they are fighting for. Let your sincere belief in yourself shine through everyday.

I can tell you that anything is possible, but ultimately, you have to believe. Tell yourself everyday that you can do it. Let your belief in yourself be a support to you. Confidence in yourself is a wonderful thing to have. Confidence in self has great value and is a very powerful element of success. Regardless of things that may have happened in your life, you have no reason to not be confident in your ability to succeed. Be confident! Be convinced! Be who you want to be.

There is only one "YOU" so be the best "YOU" that "YOU" can be.

Sacrifices

Unfortunately, getting to where you want to go in your life requires sacrifices. You have to be willing to make sacrifices in order to move forward in life. For example, recently I have decided to make moves toward a particular investment. Anyway, at the time the investment came up, I had a motorcycle that I enjoyed riding a great deal. It was a wonderful vent for me - not to mention the fact that it was something I have always wanted. As much as I enjoyed my motorcycle, I realized that it was necessary to sell it if I wanted to take steps toward my financial goals in life. I sold the motorcycle. It was not something I particularly wanted to do, but I saw it as a small sacrifice to move in the direction I wanted to go. There will be other motorcycles. I'm not saying that you should deny yourself the enjoyment of "things." Just know when it is necessary to make sacrifices of such "things" and know when it is not. Anyhow, that particular investment that stimulated the sell of my motorcycle did not work out. However, the point is that as hard as it was to let go of the bike, I had to do so if I was serious about achieving what I want out of my life. My desires lay deeper than the temporary pleasure that the motorcycle gave me. Although the investment did not work out, it was reassuring for me to know that I was willing to make such a sacrifice. Although the deal fell through, I am glad that I made the choice that I did for the mere principal it represented.

Life is full of choices and sacrifices. Sacrifices do not have to be a bad thing. If you take the time to see the positive effect that making a particular sacrifice can have, you will see that the outcome will surpass the temporary gratification of the thing or things you are sacrificing. For example, let's say you have a test tomorrow. Your friends call you and want you to go out partying with them. If you are not in school, relate this example to something of importance that could come up in your life for which you need to prepare. Anyway, knowing you have the test, you have to decide what is more important to you.

If you decide to sacrifice a night of partying to study for your test, the fulfillment you will have from doing well on your test will be much greater than the fulfillment of getting drunk will bring. If anything the gratification will be longer lasting. Chances are you may not think it is worth it when you are missing out on a good time. However, when you get your test scores back you will. This is a very simple example, but you get the point. There are always things that come up in your life that seem much more appealing than being responsible. Find the balance. Do not deprive yourself of enjoying life just make sure you make the appropriate choices when necessary.

The sacrifices one makes today can greatly increase their levels of success and achievements in the future. If you take the time to talk with people who have made it to where you want to be and will be, you will understand what it took for them to get to where they are in their lives. Moreover, I am sure that if you asked them if it was worth it, they will more than likely say, "Yes." I am not implying that you should live your life in a shell with only the future in mind. What I am suggesting is to evaluate how you spend your time. Although the future may never come, we need to be prepared if it does. Take notice as to what part of your life you think may be holding you back from stepping toward the direction you want to go and will go. You will be amazed with how good making a few small sacrifices will make you feel about the direction of your life.

Making sacrifices is a stressful and serious balancing act. You cannot sacrifice so much that you come to the point where you do not enjoy your life today. You must find the happy medium. You have to decide what you are willing to sacrifice and in what areas of your life you are not willing to make sacrifices. The important thing is to begin the process. Decide just how important your dreams are to you. Think about your life and what you can do to improve it. Remember, there is always room for improvement.

Sacrifice is an element of success. Do not miss out on what you want for yourself tomorrow because you are not willing to make the necessary sacrifices today. On the same token, tomorrow may never come, so enjoy your life today, but live it with tomorrow in mind…

Appreciate Life

One common thing that I see in today's society is a lack of appreciation. People in general tend to have a lack of appreciation for life. All to often you hear people complaining and feeling sorry for themselves. They spend a majority of their time focusing on the negative in their lives instead of focusing on the positive.

It does not matter who you are, things could always be better and things could always be worse. Life is a beautiful gift that we often take for granted. God has a plan for each one of us, and it is not for us to spend our lives focusing on negative things. Think positive. Be grateful for what you do have and seek what you want. God has blessed you with another day. Life is so precious and too quick to pass us by. It is very wise to focus on the positive things in life while using the negative things to motivate you. Though it may not seem like it, there is so much good to focus on. No matter how bad you may think you have it, if you search hard enough, you will find something to appreciate.

When I begin to feel sorry for myself or focus on nothing but the negative things in my life, I imagine others who have it worse. Most of the time I end up feeling silly for even being upset about my problems. When you take the time to be compassionate for other people's problems, you will appreciate your life a great deal more. Sometime ago, I severely broke my ankle skateboarding. Unfortunately, I had to have surgery. At first, I was very upset with the fact that it happened. I was not looking forward to being laid up on the couch for five weeks. Then I realized that I should be thankful that I have an ankle to break. There are many unfortunate people who have lost a limb or have been born without one. What right did I have to complain or be upset about my situation? Of course I had a right; I just felt unappreciative for feeling the way I did when others would give anything to have an ankle to break.

Furthermore, instead of being miserable on the couch complaining about the fact of being there, I focused on what I was supposed to gain from the whole experience. God does everything for a reason. I believe that it was a time for me to slow down, analyze my life, and think about things that I truly needed to think about. Being on the couch forced me to do so. Not only did I get a chance to think a lot through the whole experience, I also was able to see the people in my life who were there for me when it came down to it. Thank you is never enough when people go out of their way to be there for you. (You know who you are. I am forever grateful for YOU)

The truth of the matter is that there is plenty to be learned through every experience, good or bad. If you always focus on the negative things in life you may miss out on the purpose of the things that are happening. Always seek knowledge and understanding in every circumstance. Seeking lessons out of every experience is what makes a person wise. Wisdom is a great tool to possess. Seeking wisdom in your life will greatly benefit you on your journey to where you will go in your life. Be wise in all you do.

Prayer of Serenity

God grant me the serenity to accept
the things I cannot change,
Courage to change the things that I can,
And Wisdom to know the difference.

Do Not Be Afraid of Failure

In order to move forward in your life you must be willing to accept that failure is a part of it. Everyone fails at something at one point or another. The key is to not be afraid of failing. You have to look failure in the eyes and learn from it; smile at failure. Failure can be used as a lesson and a motivator if you take it the right way. The point I am trying to make is this. Do not let fear hold you back from your dreams. You have to give all you do your best, and if you fail, find out what you can do differently. Then try again, and again, and again, and again. Never let a few set backs stand in the way of where you want to go and will go in your life.

About a year and half ago I decided that I wanted to obtain a piece of rental property as an investment. You may recall the story I shared in the chapter, "Sacrifices" about me selling my motorcycle in order to be able to buy a condominium to rent. You may also remember that that particular investment did not work out. I was discouraged but was determined to reach this goal I had for myself. Over the past two years, I tried to purchase at least twenty different properties. Over and over again, the deals would fall through. Although I had all my ducks in a row and was completely qualified to make the investment, there was always some kind of a snag or hold up. Each time a property did not work the way I needed it to work for me, I would have to begin the search all over again. Frustration really began to set in. I felt like I was failing. I began to feel like I should give up. I began to ask myself, "What do I need a piece of rental property for anyway?" I had to continue to encourage myself and not let the fear of another deal failing stand in my way of what I wanted for myself. I knew deep down that I wanted to accomplish this for myself, so I did not give up.

Approximately a year and a half after beginning my journey of acquiring my first investment property, I achieved what I set out to do. I acquired my first piece of rental property. Every time I think about the property, I am so thankful that I did not give up and that I did not let the fear of everything that could go wrong with such an investment and the possibility of not being able to reach my goal hold me back from trying in the first place. Most importantly, I did not let all the failed attempts along the way prevent me from pushing forward and continuing to chase what I wanted to achieve for "me."

It is not an option to quit. Make it your way, your will; make it "you." You do not know what giving up means. The only thing you know is what you want for your life and to stay focused on your light at the end of the tunnel.

While it is very important to not give up, it is also important to understand that there are things that are just not meant to work out. There will be things that do not work out for a reason, and it does not always mean that it is a failed attempt. I am not implying to not push forward after something does not work out. Do not push something that is not meant to be pushed. You will know when things are not working out for a reason and when there is something you can do to make them work out. Pray about the decisions in your life. You will know when to stop at no costs and when you need to take a step back to see whether what you are trying for is the best for you at the time. Timing is very important. Aside from that, stay focused on what you are trying to accomplish at all times…

Stay Focused and Determined

Once you set your goals on whatever they may be, stay focused. If there is anything that is absolutely necessary to understand, it is this: there will be obstacles, nothing is easy, and you will feel like giving up more times than once. Often times, it will seem like the harder you try the harder things will get. It will seem as if your goals are not possible or realistic.

At this point you may ask yourself, "Why not just give up. I can't take it anymore. I am okay where I am at in my life; I can settle here." NO!!!! NO!!! NO!!! You can't give up! That is what the majority of the people do, and that is why the majority of people are not truly satisfied with their lives.

This is all coming to me at a point in my life where it seems like nothing but obstacles are coming at me, one after another and another. I am trying so hard to make things work, and it seems as if nothing is working. I am spending countless hours trying to make the appropriate steps to continue to move forward in my life, financially, emotionally, and spiritually. Naturally one reaches a point when he or she just feels like giving up. Do I really need to move forward in my life? The question runs through my mind. Do I need to worry about all the things I am worrying about?

Through all the smoke, I know it will clear; things will work out. If I continue to spend my time wisely and make good choices and the appropriate sacrifices, things will fall into place. My determination will allow things to work out and so will yours.

As I am determined to not give up, you can not either. If I can do it, you can too. Stay focused. Keep your sights on what you want to achieve. When you feel like you are running out of gas, dig deep and find your desires; find your drive to succeed. Think about your goals. Analyze your views of the future and what you want out of it.

This is your life. You have to live your life. Do not let any obstacles stand in the way of making the best out of your life. You will not see the end of the show if you turn off the T.V.

Always Take the Time to Appreciate Your Accomplishments Along the Way

As you begin to make progress on your journey and begin to accomplish the things you desire for yourself, always remember to take the time to reflect on your achievements. Reflect on what you have done. Remember what you have had to overcome to get to where you are. No matter where you are in your life, you have still had to overcome many obstacles to get there. No matter how big or small you think your achievements are, they are of great proportion. Life is filled with an abundance of adversities. It is not something that can be breezed through without any difficult times. To "be" is an accomplishment in itself. To be here today, taking the time to read this book, to be able to read, it all means something.

Never be discouraged by the fact that someone else is where you want to be and you are not there yet. You will get "there" if that is where you want to go. Everyone is placed in certain circumstances for a reason - to make them who they are meant to be. If you continue to stay focused and determined, everything will come in time. Appreciate where "you" are in your life and do not stress out over where someone else is in his or her life. Believe me, I know how terribly hard this is to do. This was and still is very difficult for me. I am a highly competitive person. I strive to be the best in whatever I do. When I began to see other people reach goals I have for myself, I saw no reason why they should be there and I should not. I would start to get very hard on myself. I immediately thought I was doing something wrong. I had to make conscious efforts to focus on my own life.

However, I do seek knowledge from what someone else has accomplished. Try to understand what they have done wrong and right, so you can learn from them. I am not saying to not let these people motivate you. It is okay to get worked up. You have to see that you can be there. It is just a matter of time. Be patient. All good things come in time. This is hard to accept; one of the hardest. Naturally, you are going to get irritated. You know what you want; you will get it. The bottom line is to not hate on others for what they have that you want; just work harder to achieve what you want. If you are not at where you want to be at in your life and where you feel like you should be, stop and think what is holding you back and what you can do differently. Ask yourself, "Do I have control over why I am not 'there.'" Focus! See your sights; forget about whether you are on schedule or not. Move forward, get "it" together, and do "it"...

Never Forget Where You Come From and Always Remember the Ones Who Have Helped You Along The Way

As you take your journey toward reaching your goals, there will be many bends in the road. With those bends there will be many people that will help you. God will put people in your life to help you through each season. Focus on those people who are trying to help you. As you begin to look back on your life, no matter how young or old you may be, think about those who have helped you - the ones who have been there for you when you needed them. Always take the time to thank people for their kindness as well as their guidance. Never forget where you come from and who you came with.

There are many people who have had a positive impact on my life. I will never forget those people. I am forever grateful for those who have helped me. I would not be who I am today if it was not for "those" very important people in my life. “Those” people will always hold a special place in my heart. Be aware of when God may be trying to put someone in your life for a reason. There is a reason for everything.

There will be people in your life will help you along the way. Some may help big some may help small, but in the end it all adds up to the person you will become through the kindness of others and the determination within yourself. While it is important to recognize the people who have helped you along the way it is equally as important to give to someone what has been given to you. This help I speak of is not relying on others to do for you or you do another person’s job for them, it is as simple as a kind word of encouragement. It is the little things that add up to the big things.

Although you may feel like you are alone and may very well be, think real deeply and you will see that you have been helped more than you may know. I have always felt alone. I have felt like I was in a battle with one sword against a whole army. However, as I look back I can now appreciate the few that have been there for me. Like I said, it is those few that have made all the difference in my life. To me, the few are millions in relation to how grateful I am for them. Be grateful for each and every person who has helped you. IF you are at a point in your life where you cannot speak of anyone who has helped you in some way, God will send you someone. Be alert, until he does know he is there, his footprints are right beside yours.

Conclusion

We all have our own desires burning inside of us. There is such a wide variety of personalities and of goals people have for themselves. The individuality of each one of us will cause us to have a different experience of life. Although we may be exposed to similar circumstances, we will all take something different away from "it."

What may make one of us happy, will not make the other equally as happy. Focus on "you." Know what "you" want for your life. Set "your" goals and chase "your" dreams. Continue to grow in yourself on a daily basis. Do not settle in any part of your life. Get what you want out of life. Keep your priorities in the right places.

God has given us life so get all the joys and beauty that we are all meant to get out of "it." You will have good as well as bad times. Always remember, someone has it worse. Do not let anything hold you back or let time pass you by.

Be your life and grow with your time. Get out of your life what you are meant to have, HAPPINESS…

Closing Statement

I hope that you are able to take something positive from this book. Regardless of where you are in you life or what your desires may be for yourself, I know you will do well. I wish you all the blessings in life you deserve.

Contact Ricky Roberts at

TATE PUBLISHING, LLC

127 East Trade Center Terrace

Mustang, Oklahoma 73064

(888) 361-9473

TATE PUBLISHING, LLC

www.tatepublishing.com